5 Prayers for Business That Get Results

Bob Perry & Amy Joy Lykosh

MAKARIOS
PRESS

Esmont, VA

Makarios Press
P.O. Box 28, Esmont, VA 22937

© 2021 by Bob Perry and Amy Joy Lykosh

All rights reserved. No part of this book may be reproduced in any form except in the case of brief quotations without written permission from Makarios Press.

Order reprints of this booklet at amazon.com, or contact Amy directly for bulk pricing. Amy@workplaceprayer.com.

Scripture in NIV unless otherwise stated.

Design: Nate Braxton

ISBN 978-1-956561-07-4

Printed in the United States of America

CONTENTS

Prologue 5

Prayer 1: Pray for Progress 7

Prayer 2: Pray for Perception 9

Prayer 3: Pray for Production 11

Prayer 4: Pray for Provision 13

Prayer 5: Pray for Practicalities 15

Epilogue 19

PROLOGUE

At Workplace Prayer, we pray for businesses and teach people in the workplace how to pray effectively.

For over four decades, managing director Bob Perry has had a single-minded pursuit: *Lord, teach me to pray.*

After thousands of prayer meetings and tens of thousands of hours, Bob has found the best method of prayer.

The problem: it's easy to discount or overlook.

It seems too familiar, too simple.

It's not.

Think of the power of certain words: *I love you. I hate you.*

Now multiply that power with the power of God, the same power that raised Jesus from the dead.

Hebrews 4:12 says, "For the word of God is alive and active. Sharper than any double-edged sword, it penetrates even to dividing soul and spirit, joints and marrow; it judges the thoughts and attitudes of the heart."

Want the most powerful prayers possible?

Pray the scriptures.

We'll model our method in these prayers to come.

Since prayer is one of the secret weapons of acceleration for the kingdom of God in the workplace, we are excited for you to pray more effectively over your business.

And if you ever have any questions about prayer in the workplace, since prayer is our passion and vocation, we would be delighted to talk to you. You can find us at **workplaceprayer.com**.

— Bob & Amy

Prayer 1
PRAY FOR PROGRESS
God Grants This Request

Look at this four part, bold prayer from I Chronicles 4:10: *Jabez cried out to the God of Israel, "Oh, that you would bless me and enlarge my territory! Let your hand be with me, and keep me from harm so that I will be free from pain." And God granted his request.*

Jabez did not pray a calm, dispassionate request. He *cried out!*

Bob describes this as a pounding on the table prayer: "I'm not letting up until I see significant answers! I need a breakthrough!"

We pray this almost daily for our clients, because we know that when we get a breakthrough, our breakthrough blesses others.

When Thomas Edison got his breakthrough in lighting, his breakthrough changed the world.

When William Wilberforce got his breakthrough in England, enslaved people worldwide shared his triumph as they went free.

When God spoke to Abram, he called him out of his

homeland, promising him:

"I will make you into a great nation, and I will bless you; I will make your name great, and you will be a blessing. I will bless those who bless you, and whoever curses you I will curse; and all peoples on earth will be blessed through you" (Genesis 12:2-3).

Did you catch that? When God blessed Abraham, it wasn't so that he could keep all the blessing for himself; he blessed him to bless others!

So as the Lord blesses you and increases your influence and impact, you then get to be the conduit of blessing to those around you!

Your breakthrough can shift daily life and the history of the nations of the earth.

It's good to pound the table ... because the world still awaits breakthrough in many places.

———·✦·———

Lord, I ask that you would bless me indeed. Bless me altogether.

Enlarge my influence. Enlarge my territory.

And when you answer those requests, Lord, and the results feel overwhelming, then may your hand be with me, to guide, protect, comfort, and direct.

And through it all, Lord, keep me from harm of all types. Keep me from the evil one and from malice, and keep me from accidents and disasters.

Thank you, Lord, that your word says that you answered this request for Jabez, and so I ask that you do it again for me.

Prayer 2
PRAY FOR PERCEPTION
The Glorious Father Gives Wisdom

Bob teaches that, if you ever need to pray a prayer and you aren't sure what to pray, Ephesians 1:17 is always a great choice: *I keep asking that the God of our Lord Jesus Christ, the glorious Father, may give you the Spirit of wisdom and revelation, so that you may know him better.*

This prayer is very important for all in the workplace: for the entrepreneur, for the CEO, for someone wanting to write a book, someone that feels there are inventions in them, that there are things that they're called to create.

The Ephesians 1:17 prayer brings insight and perception. It's like night vision: it gives you the ability to see more than what you know.

It gives you the ability to feel and discern. Romans 14:17 says that the kingdom of God is righteousness, peace, and joy in the Holy Spirit.

Two out of three—peace and joy!—are feelings or emotions.

Part of the upgrade of Ephesians 1:17 is that you begin to recognize how God speaks to you, giving you supernatural intelligence, discernment, and wisdom.

In the daily fog of life, this prayer helps break through the cloudy conditions.

It's a storage bank into the necessary wisdom when you don't know what to do, or where to go, when all else has failed.

The Passion Translation reads: "I pray that the Father of glory, the God of our Lord Jesus Christ, would impart to you the riches of the Spirit of wisdom and the Spirit of revelation to know him through your deepening intimacy with him."

Paul seeks to impart these riches: not only to communicate, but also to bestow, to give.

Pray big, pray big, pray big. God has plans and purposes that he wants to reveal to you.

The infinite wise God desires to give you ideas. The infinite wise one, the Everlasting Father, desires to give you the plans, the book, the blueprint that will impact people's lives.

Pray big. The spirit of wisdom and revelation is upon you.

This prayer brings results now, but in the beauty of God's abundance, it also offers long-term benefits, like a time release capsule.

This prayer is good any time, and in any season, but especially when you're starting something, or when your back's against the wall, or when you need breakthrough.

Lord, may I walk with peace and confidence, even in the delays in my life. Thank you for the partnership in intercession with the Holy Spirit, the divine helper, who reveals God's unfailing purposes. Thank you that I walk in God's love as his beloved joy.

Lord, I desire your wisdom and revelation, your knowledge and enlightenment. Release your riches, Father of glory. Amen.

Prayer 3
PRAY FOR PRODUCTION
Because We All Need Wisdom

The prophet said of Jesus in Isaiah 11:2: *The Spirit of the Lord will rest on him—the Spirit of wisdom and of understanding, the Spirit of counsel and of might, the Spirit of the knowledge and fear of the Lord.*

What a prophecy!

Amy once asked Bob, "Is it okay to pray for this for me? I don't want to overreach, since Isaiah said this of Jesus."

Bob said, "Paul said in I Corinthians 2:16 that we have the mind of Christ, and Jesus himself said in John 14:12 that we will do greater works than he did. So pray it for yourself! Absolutely!"

Well ... that blew open the doors of possibility!

Our client Gilbert Hintz, a large-scale organic farmer, read this same verse in the New English Translation and adopted it as his life verse, at least in this season.

The Lord's Spirit will rest on him—a Spirit that gives extraordinary wisdom, a Spirit that provides the ability to execute plans, a Spirit that produces absolute loyalty to the Lord.

So often in business we have good ideas, but then we don't know how to execute them with excellence.

———•✸•———

Oh, Lord, I need wisdom, far more than I have. Thank you for the promise in James 1:5 that I can ask with eager and confident expectation that you will give wisdom as often as I ask.

Thank you.

And, Lord, I want your extraordinary wisdom, combined with the ability to execute plans. Yes, Lord! Pour that out! I want to be absolutely loyal to you, Lord.

Teach me your ways, and let me walk in your will. May I be effective in your kingdom.

Thank you, Lord. In Jesus' name, amen.

Prayer 4
PRAY FOR PROVISION
God Is a God of Plenty

Deuteronomy 8:18 is one of the best prayers to pray over your business. *But remember the LORD your God, for it is he who gives you the ability to produce wealth, and so confirms his covenant, which he swore to your ancestors, as it is today.*

From its founding in 1990, the homeschool company Sonlight Curriculum offered morning prayer meetings, on the clock, for their staff.

Thirty years later, the owners hired Bob to pray.

Within a few months, they were amazed at the increase.

President Sarita Holzmann said, "For thirty years, we have prayed for our customers, for our staff, for our vendors, for our materials, for the unreached peoples of the world ... but I never once thought to pray for increase."

But why wouldn't the Lord want to bless his children with increase?

Kris Vallotton, in teaching on the last chapter of John, pointed out that, when the disciples cast out their nets and couldn't haul them in because they were so full, that bounty, that abundance, that over-the-top provision was the sign to

John that Jesus was the one who spoke to them.

He didn't say, "Oh! Here's a minnow, so at least we won't starve. Must be the Lord."

No. Jesus' abundant provision pointed to who he was.

As business owners, and as people of prayer, we want to call out for all the blessings the Lord has for us.

Lord, thank you that your word says that you are the one who gives the ability to produce wealth. So I'm asking for financial increase. Your word says this, so as one of your children, seeking to make a difference in your kingdom, please do what you say.

I am asking, Lord, that you would indeed confirm the covenant.

I'm asking, Lord, that you would expose the things that need to be exposed in order to drive out unrighteousness. Lord, for your righteous ones, I'm asking for your clarity and your direction and your purpose.

I am asking, Lord, that as you press on us, that if dross comes out in the beginning, that what would come out in the end would be oil, or would be grape juice that would age into the finest wine.

Lord, may we be productive in your kingdom.

May we be productive, Lord, for your name's sake.

We cry with the saints of old, with our brothers and sisters around the world: may the Lamb who was slain receive the full reward for his suffering! Amen!

Prayer 5
PRAY FOR PRACTICALITIES
Jesus Taught This

Almost the first day they met, Bob said to Amy: "Prayer works. Otherwise, why would we bother praying?"

Think about this. Do you believe that your prayers make a difference? Do you believe that God answers?

Think of the Lord's Prayer in Matthew 6:9-13. (KJV)

Our Father which art in heaven, Hallowed be thy name.

This prayer begins with praise, but then transitions immediately into requests.

Thy kingdom come, Thy will be done in earth, as it is in heaven.

An enormous first request: we want earth to look like heaven.

Heaven has no injustice, no poverty, no pain, no miscommunication, no fear.

Instead, it is so full of glory that the streets are paved with gold, and all the creatures worship the Lamb that was slain.

So if you're ever not sure what to pray, you can always pray for your life and your work to be a picture of God's kingdom and will.

Give us this day our daily bread.

Think of how practical this request is.

When the disciples asked for daily bread, they expected to have daily bread.

They didn't wonder if maybe today they would ask, but go hungry.

No. They expected that when they asked, they would be satisfied.

When you pray the scriptures, this can be your posture in prayer, too. Pray for the details, and expect answers.

And forgive us our debts, as we forgive our debtors.

This part of the prayer may seem less practical than "Give us this day our daily bread," except this prayer covers human relationships.

And since business runs on relationships, this request is incredibly pertinent to business owners. It's a way of saying, "Keep us right before you and others. When others hurt us, may we not hold that against them."

And lead us not into temptation, but deliver us from evil.

When you pray this, you should expect that God is able to keep temptation and evil away from you, that God is strong enough to protect you.

For thine is the kingdom, and the power, and the glory, for ever. Amen.

And as this beautiful prayer ends, God owns the kingdom, and all power, and deserves all glory, both now and into eternity.

The Lord's prayer: so simple, so beautiful, and so all encompassing.

Here's a testimony of a short prayer's answer.

One fall day, Amy was out walking and praying for a client in the midst of the harvest season. She recorded a quick prayer on several topics, including the line, "Lord, be with the harvesters. We know that big equipment always has an element of danger, so keep them safe."

She sent off the recording and went about her day.

Days later, the client emailed her: "[Our farm manager] got caught in the potato digger chain—doesn't know how he got out! It should have taken his head off. (His words.) This was the same timing of your urgent feeling to pray about safety. A God moment for sure."

Prayer works. Otherwise, why bother?

———•✶•———

Jesus, I thank you that in your prayer I see no sense of confusion, but only full confidence that this prayer will be efficacious.

Thank you that this is not some sort of theoretical, "wouldn't it be nice?" prayer, but rather an on-point, practical prayer, in which the disciples expected that you would answer their requests in power.

Lord, I am asking that you would give me that same sense of expectation that what I say to you matters in this earth. Thank you that when you speak your words to me, I get to speak them back to you in faith, and that you are able to accomplish your plans through me.

Lord, I am asking for an upgrade in understanding and ability, that you would be exalted in my life, and that your name would be exalted in this earth.

In the name of Jesus, amen.

EPILOGUE

Once Amy was talking to a friend, a Forbes Top 100 Wealth Manager. He told about an interaction with a client who mentioned, in the course of an appointment, that he hired young prostitutes in Las Vegas.

Amy's friend said, "Why are you doing that? They are the age of your daughters!"

The client replied, "That's what makes it good."

Amy looked at her friend, stunned.

She had no idea this was part of his workday ... or anyone's workday.

"Who is covering you in prayer when you go into the pit of hell like that?"

He said, "I have some friends who pray."

"Do they pray more than a sentence a week?"

"Oh! I don't know!"

And so Workplace Prayer acquired a client.

Hopefully you are not dealing with anything quite so blatantly exploitive and wicked.

But the reality is: as a person in the workplace, you deal with challenges every day.

You need:
- Direction
- Wisdom
- Easing of relationships between staff members
- Legal protection
- Energy and strength for the journey
- And on and on....

Who is covering you and your business in prayer?

At Workplace Prayer, we know that focused, intentional prayer produces results.

We spend hours each day in prayer, interceding for our clients. Hours in worship and praise, in tears and groans, in celebration of testimonies, and intercession for breakthrough.

We also know that spiritual gifts come in both general and specific forms.

All believers should seek to bear one another's burdens, but not all believers are called to be pastors.

All believers should be ready to give a reason for the hope that is in them with meekness and fear, but not all believers have the gift of evangelism.

All believers should pray, but not all believers have the gift of prayer—the desire and drive to pray for extended periods of time, and to see powerful breakthrough in financial and other areas.

Beyond that, at Workplace Prayer, we recognize that prayer works most effectively in partnership.

Yes, Jesus went off by himself to pray at times, but the night before his crucifixion, at the moment of his most intense need, he invited others to join with him.

Think of the 120 in the upper room in Acts 1 and 2, praying constantly, until the Holy Spirit came on them.

Think of Paul and Silas in the prison in Philippi, singing together into the night, when an earthquake shook the prison and they could escape.

The record of the scripture is that partnership in prayer produces powerful results.

We pray individually, yes, but we also pray corporately, every day. We want all the acceleration possible for you and your business.

Lord, your word says in Deuteronomy 32:30, "How could one man chase a thousand, or two put ten thousand to flight, unless their Rock had sold them, unless the LORD had given them up?"

Lord, I cry out for the benefit of praying in partnership. I thank you that one can put a thousand to flight, but I cry out even more for the multiplication in results that comes with praying in partnership.

Teach me, Lord, to pray after your pattern. Jesus, as you prayed in the Lord's Prayer only "we" and "our" words, and no "I" and "me" words. Teach me what it means to pray in unity and with power.

Teach me to pray.

Thank you, Lord.

ABOUT THE AUTHORS

Bob Perry has been a passionate student of prayer for more than four decades, constantly asking, "Lord, teach me to pray." He has founded and led multiple prayer initiatives that have trained and mobilized hundreds of thousands of people in prayer partnerships.

Amy Joy Lykosh loves healing and deliverance. Her heart's cry comes from the verse, "My people are destroyed for lack of knowledge" (Hosea 4:6). The author of several highly acclaimed books, she seeks to stop the destruction as best she can through writing and speaking.

Together, they run Workplace Prayer, to cover businesses in prayer, and Prayer Mentoring, to raise up healthy intercessors to bring the kingdom of God to bear in their lives and communities.

Be in your happy place.

AS IT IS IN HEAVEN
Why Workplace Prayer Exists

When Jesus taught on prayer, he began, "Our Father in heaven, hallowed be your name, your kingdom come, your will be done, on earth as it is in heaven." How can we effectively pray God's kingdom on earth, if we don't know what heaven looks like? If we want to pray better, we need to understand what we're praying for. Catch a glimpse of heaven in these short free verse poems, taken from Revelation 4 and 5. Pressed for time? You could read a single chapter. Or even a single poem!

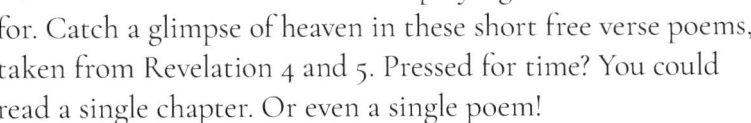

> "I just sat down with your book. I am on the second page. In tears. Thank you. Beautiful and song-like. And fun." — **Sarah**

> "I feel like each line of each poem is like a choice morsel of truth that I just want to savor slowly. I set aside your book to read in quiet and cozy moments wrapped in a quilt on my bed. It is something I look forward to and cherish." — **Elena**

> "I love the short meditative chapters. It's great bedtime reading. Congratulations!!" — **Perry Marshall**

FIND OUT MORE AT
makariospress.com/heaven

ORDER AT
amazon.com

THE PRINCE PROTECTS HIS CITY
Nehemiah Prayed Four Months, Then Rebuilt the Wall in Only 52 Days

Such a great story! But how easy to miss!

Nehemiah wasn't a warrior or a king. He was a tremendous administrator, a gifted leader, a world-class historian, a treasured friend, a successful fundraiser, and a prince. Though he was never a CEO, he headed an enormous public works project he had planned, then served as governor for twelve years. And he prayed constantly. A free verse look at the book of Nehemiah. Come meet a man who brought God's kingdom to bear in his work.

> "I finished reading it today! Loved it. Such a nice quick pace to read Nehemiah and also space to sit in parts if I just wanted to read one page" — **Angela**

FIND OUT MORE AT
makariospress.com/the-prince-protects-his-city

ORDER AT
amazon.com

GROW WITH PRAYER EXPERIENCES

Throughout the year, we offer a wide range of prayer experiences: Communal Fasts, Prayer Challenges, and Sacred Assemblies.

If you want to grow in prayer in creative and unexpected ways, come join us.

FIND OUT MORE AT
PrayerExperiences.com

ONE VOICE: THE STORY OF WILLIAM WILBERFORCE
Gorgeous Story of Tenacity + Courage

Biography in verse of the man who, despite all obstacles, fought to end the Slave Trade in Great Britain. Powerful story of tenacity and courage.

> "I think it's important to know Wilberforce's story, but One Voice has become one of my absolute favourite books of all time and is SO worth buying just for the beautiful writing. I was so skeptical when I first opened it and realized it was written in free verse but oh, it's so, so special. I can't make it through without sobbing." — **Emily**

ORDER EXCLUSIVELY AT
sonlight.com

---

21 DAYS OF A F(E)AST
A Fast That Feels More Like a Feast

Why fasting is a joy, and why you should do it. A guide for a fast that anyone can do, even if you can't restrict calories. The four types of fasting, and how to choose. Morning and evening readings for 21 days. Stories and testimonies. Drawn from four decades of experience and wisdom. Come sit in the Lord's presence.

> "Appreciating the wealth within this book!! Such a brilliant resource!" — **Nicole**

ORDER AT
amazon.com

PRAYER REFRESH
Short Prayers to Pray Through Your Day

You don't have to completely change your life, your habits, your personality, or your social media usage in order to have a good prayer life.

This book introduces a wide variety of prayers that you can pray in a minute or less, that will fit into your day, right where you are. Don't start with hours on your knees. Start with the stray half minutes here and there. Use it as a devotional for 21 days, or read straight through.

> "The Prayer Refresh was so life changing, perspective shattering, and breathed so much, much needed life into me and our home that I long to go through it again. Regularly. Like monthly." — **Amanda**

ORDER AT amazon.com

JUNETEENTH: AN INVITATION TO FAST
Both the Why and the How To

Join us in a one-day fast.

> "The booklet was so helpful with the historical summary of the date (which I knew nothing about), as well as specific prayers and family examples, to guide my focused petitions. The format is beautiful, and so clearly organized! Great resource!" — **Eileen**

ORDER AT amazon.com

Made in the USA
Monee, IL
13 April 2022